THE YOUNG SPORTSMAN'S GUIDE TO
CAMPING

THE
YOUNG SPORTSMAN'S GUIDE
TO
CAMPING

by

John L. Holden

WITH PHOTOGRAPHS BY EDWARD BETZ

Galahad Books • New York City

Acknowledgments

The author wishes to express his grateful appreciation to:

The men and boys with whom he has had the privilege of camping through many wonderful years. Without their enthusiasm and their comradery the experience so essential to the development of this book might never have been gained.

The late Bernard S. Mason, one of the truly great campers and woodsmen of our time, for his inspiration, understanding, and teaching in youthful years.

The men of *Kooch-i-ching,* whose loyal and untiring efforts have contributed so handsomely to a developing wealth of camping information.

The campers who appear in the photographs taken especially for this book: John Keller, Tom Smith, Dan Shick, John Spencer, Scott MacAllister, Terry Hess, Steve Bryant, Clint Frank, John Berry, Steve Collett, Bob Cowden, Tom Vandenbark, Nelson Spencer, Dick Wagner, Steve Robins, Brad Shinkle, Phil Grout, Foster Gamble, John McArthur, Laird Davis, Dave Eustice, Larry Terhune, Bill Ohl, Steve Fast, Doug Eustice and Tim Heinle.

Contents

WANT TO BE A CAMPER!

Have you ever felt the urge to leave your home in the city and head for the open country or the woods with a pack on your back and a song in your heart, to meet the challenge and find the adventure of living and traveling in the great outdoors? You have! Then you want to be a camper. Have you ever thought you might like to pack some clothing and equipment in the family car and start on a trip to Yellowstone Park or the Tetons, to Grand Canyon or the Blue Ridge Mountains, to the lakes of Maine or the Everglades of Florida? You have! Then you want to be a camper. Every true camper dreams of the fabulous trips he will take, of the mountains he will climb, of the prairies he will cross on horseback, of the rapids he will shoot. He looks forward to the day when he may find himself standing on the rocky shore of a lake far away in the great north woods where the water shimmers in the sun light and sparkles like a sea of blue diamonds; where the air is so fresh and clear that he breathes deeply to fill his lungs with its pure goodness; where he may smell the fragrant incense of spruce and balsam trees and listen at night for the haunting laugh of loons across the water; where he may pitch his tent on the soft pine needles of the forest floor and sleep that wonderful restful sleep which city dwellers never know. He dreams of these adventures and many more, and he finds the fun and joy of camping close to home too. To him any patch of woods will do, and every season is camping season.

If you want to be a camper you will want to learn the woods-wise ways of camping so that you may camp in comfort and safety like an old-timer and not rough it like a tenderfoot. This book is written to help you learn how to camp properly and find the fun and thrill of real camping at its very best.

LIKE THE INDIAN

History tells us that our pioneer ancestors were good campers; they had to be in order to survive. It also tells us that they learned camping from those master campers of all times, the American Indians.

Many of the things our forefathers learned about camping from the Indians are good medicine today, just as they were hundreds of years ago. If you had a chance to learn something from an old, old Indian you would probably find that the good camper is a cautious and careful person, that he leaves nothing to chance, that he avoids mistakes like the plague and plans everything carefully for he knows that his comfort and his safety will depend upon good planning.

You would learn that a first-rate camper has endless patience, that he always shows respect for his fellow campers, that he is ever helpful and seldom critical, that he is always willing to do more than his share of the work, for this spirit is the spirit which makes camping so worthwhile.

You would learn that the real camper takes good care of his equipment and the equipment of others, that he is never careless, that he takes great pride in being a neat, clean, and orderly person, that he takes exceptional pride in the condition of his knife and ax, for these are the badge of his woodsmanship.

Most important, you would learn that the good camper is the person with whom other people want to camp. You can receive no greater compliment from a good camper than his request to go camping with you.

THEN DRESS FOR CAMP LIVING

Nothing will contribute more to your comfort and health as a camper than proper clothing for fair weather and foul, for hot weather and cold; and nothing will arouse more controversy among seasoned campers than a lively discussion about camp clothing. The woodsiest of the old-timers will agree that your clothes should keep you clean and comfortable, warm and dry; and they should provide adequate protection for you at all times. They should be as light and compact as possible.

Take a look at the camper here. He is returning to his campsite from an afternoon in the woods. He is clothed properly with a pair of leather shoes, wool sox, undershorts, a long-sleeved shirt, long pants, and a hat. His clothing has given him protection from the underbrush and the insects, yet it is light enough to be comfortable.

When the day is hot and the sun is bright, and you are eager to soak up some of that medicine from the sky like the sun-bronzed camper on the opposite page, you will need only the bare essentials in the way of clothing: a pair of light shoes and shorts. But be careful; don't overdo it. Before that tan becomes a burn put on your long pants and a shirt. Play it safe.

When clouds move in and rain threatens it's time to don your rain gear. The wet weather camper you see opposite has put on rubber-bottom boots, rain pants, and rain parka. He knows that the wise camper is the dry one.

A bit of experience and individual taste will lead you to your own best camping wardrobe, but until you gain that experience you will find the following guide practical.

Shoes—Good comfortable shoes are more important to the camper than any other part of his clothing. For general camping you will want a pair of tennis shoes, a pair of light leather shoes or moccasin-pac shoes, and a pair of light rubber-bottom, leather-top boots about ten inches high. If you hike you will need a pair of sturdy leather shoes or leather boots about six inches high which fit perfectly. If you hunt, climb mountains, ride horses, or tramp through the snow you will need special footwear. Do not go without it.

Sox—Wool sox or those made of a blend of wool and synthetic fibers are accepted universally, and in all instances they are best. At least two pairs are needed.

Underclothing—At least two sets of underclothing are a must, and they should match the weather. Cotton shorts and T shirts or a wool-cotton blend are best for the warm days. Insulated longies are a must for cold weather camping.

Pants—Your pants should be sturdy and serviceable, for they will take a beating. Twill or khaki shorts with pockets are right for warm weather; and you should have a pair of heavy blue denim or other sturdy cotton long pants for protection against sun, wind, cold, and insects. Woolen stag pants are great for winter.

Shirts—The wool shirt is the camper's shirt. It is sturdy, comfortable, warm, dries quickly, and makes a good pad. It should be supplemented with T shirts, sweat shirts, or flannel shirts. Sweaters? Only in the mountains. For extra warmth put your shirts on in layers.

Jackets—Not needed in summer, a jacket is a must in the fall. A poplin or synthetic jacket with synthetic fleece lining is excellent. A light and sturdy wool jacket is great. Heavy jackets are an abomination.

Hats—When you camp you will need a hat for sun and rain protection if for no other reason. An old felt hat is fine. For added comfort remove the sweat band and replace it with a leather thong around the base of the crown to hold the hat in shape. A baseball cap will do.

Belts—Take a sturdy leather one. Besides holding up your pants it will prove useful in many other ways.

Rain clothing—The two-piece rain suit is best for the camper. A poncho is good. A raincoat will suffice. Be sure you have adequate rain clothing.

Gloves—Buckskin gloves are tops for camping. Cotton work gloves will do the job too. And when the days turn cold you will want a pair of wool-lined mittens like the ones the cold weather camper is wearing here.

SELECT THE RIGHT EQUIPMENT

Want to be a successful camper and a comfortable one? Then learn this secret. Select your equipment carefully; learn to use it well, and take everything you need but not one item more. You may learn something of value from this camper. He displays the things he has selected for a short trip through the north woods by foot and canoe.

He is wearing tennis shoes, wool sox, undershorts, a T shirt, shorts, and a belt. He will pack his Duluth Pack with a sleeping bag, air mattress, moccasin-pacs, blue jeans, small towel, wool shirt, sweat shirt, bandana, extra sox, undershorts and T shirt, toilet kit, tarp, maps and compass, rubber bags, plastic bags, gloves, flashlight, knife stone, ax stone, waterproof match safe, notebook and pencil, first-aid kit, needle and thread, film, skillet, pot, plate, cup, fork and spoon, rope, ax and sheath, saw and sheath, and rain parka. He will carry a canteen, sheath knife, pocketknife, whistle on lanyard, and a camera. He is well equipped for the job ahead.

YOUR KNIVES

Did you know that a good knife is the number one tool of a good camper? You can always distinguish the experienced campers from the tenderfeet by the knives they carry. From the hundreds of knives available you will want to select one or two which will do a job for you.

Your first knife should be a pocketknife of sturdy construction with at least one keen blade for whittling. A quality jackknife will do. A scout knife is better because of its varied blades and many uses. The Swiss army knife can not be beat. As a second knife select a sheath knife of good quality with a thin blade about four and one-half to five inches long. This is the knife for preparing meals, cleaning fish, and skinning game. Many manufacturers make knives which fit this description. The camper's knife supreme is Gerber's Shorty. No clumsy hunting knives, sabers, bayonets, or machetes please! They are all utterly worthless for campers and exceptionally dangerous in the woods.

KEEN AND CLEAN

Few things are more useless or dangerous than dull knives. Your fine knives merit fine care. You can keep them clean with a bit of scouring powder, protected with a few drops of oil, and sharp with a pocket stone like the one in the illustration.

To sharpen your knife moisten the stone with a few drops of water, hold it firmly on a flat surface between your thumb and fingers, and grind the edge of your knife blade on it using a circular motion. Careful! Don't cut your fingers. Keep the back of the blade elevated a few degrees and grind the entire cutting edge evenly. Grind first one side and then the other, switching frequently. It may take quite a while to sharpen a dull knife, but once you have it sharp a few minutes of additional honing after each use will keep it that way. If you are looking for that razor edge, just strop your knife on an old leather belt or strap. And remember, a knife will grow dull without that stone to keep it sharp.

CUTS AND SHORT CUTS

As the old-timers who sat around the potbellied stove in the country store knew, it's loads of fun to whittle. You will find that whittling is not only fun but also a very practical skill for the camper. When you become proficient with your knife, you will be able to make rustic furnishings, grills, snares, skewers, toaster sticks, and many other gadgets and contrivances.

The camper on page 16 is using the basic whittling grip. His fingers encircle the haft of his knife, and his thumb locks them in place. He is cutting with a firm hand and steady pressure down into the wood as well as away from himself. Long cuts call for steady strokes which cut long smooth shavings.

The camper on the opposite page is demonstrating two additional whittling techniques. In the upper picture he is using his knife as a drawknife. This gives him the control necessary to smooth out those preliminary rough cuts. He is whittling toward himself. To do this safely he must keep his wrist stiff, grip tight, elbow close to his waist, and exert steady pressure with his arm. In the lower picture he is trimming an exact cut. He gains sure control of his knife by steadying it with his right hand while he exerts all of the cutting pressure with his left thumb.

When you want to make a large notch in a piece of wood, start with a small notch and whittle the sides away until you have a large one. To cut a stick in two make a series of small notches around the stick until it parts. When you trim the twigs from a branch, start at the base and trim toward the tip. This way you will avoid splintering the branch.

And don't! Don't whittle buildings or furniture. Don't cut live trees, wire, or metal. Don't open cans with your knife. Don't throw or stick your knife in the ground. Respect your knife, care for it, and it will give you years of good service.

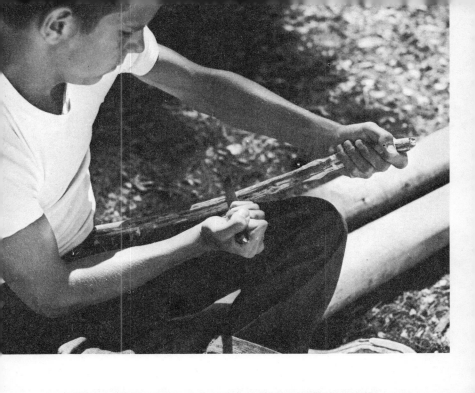

NOW FOR AN AX

When you graduate from the status of camper to that of woodsman you will undoubtedly take great pride in a collection of fine axes and your ability to use them all, but as a camper you will be interested primarily in small axes suitable for camping. You may start with a hand ax such as the scout ax, or the excellent Marble #9, then move on to a camp ax with its 20-inch handle and 20-ounce head, or the famous pound and a half Hudson Bay ax with its 24-inch handle, or the popular three-quarter pole ax which weighs two pounds.

The illustration shows a camper using his Hudson Bay to split a billet of wood. The other axes are on display from left to right, and also a full pole ax which is used for chopping, a cruiser's ax, and the full double-bit ax of the logger.

Your ax is almost indispensable in the woods. Keep it in topnotch shape. Take pride in it and never lend it to anyone. You are not expected to; it is personal property. And do not ask another camper for his ax. Bad manners, you know! It just isn't done.

SHARP, SHEATHED, AND HANDLED

A dull ax, a loose head, an uncovered blade—all are dangerous. Your ax should be sharp, tight of head, well hung, and sheathed when not in use. It is the badge of your woodsmanship.

Handle loose! Then soak the head in a bucket of water overnight. This should tighten it. If not, a new handle may be in order.

No sheath! Then have your local harnessmaker or shoemaker fashion one for you like the one pictured here.

Now let's sharpen that ax so that it will sing. You will need a mill file, a round ax stone, and a pair of gloves. Hold the ax securely in one hand, and rest the blade on your knee as the camper has done in the illustration. With a glove on your other hand to protect your fingers, grasp the mill file firmly and push a series of short strokes toward the ax blade. Keep the file at a slight and constant angle with the blade and push, do not pull.

Turn the ax over and repeat the process on the other side. Now moisten the surface of your ax stone and hone both edges of the ax blade using a circular motion. Keep the stone at the same angle with the blade as you did the file. After each use hone your ax with the stone, and this will keep it sharp and ready for work.

21

CHOP, CHOP

As you learn to use your ax listen to it occasionally, for it is said that a real woodsman can "make his ax talk." Now, shake hands with your hand ax, and you have the proper grip. Swing it with a full arm motion and you have the right stroke, a long and forceful one.

To chop a small stick hold it against the edge of a chopping block or a log and strike it at this point of contact with a slanting blow of 45 degrees like the camper pictured here. Do this properly, and a good bite will result with no kickback of the stick. To split this stick in half raise ax and stick together; then strike both together. Do not chop *at* the stick with your ax. To split a larger piece of wood stand it on end, place the bit of your ax on it, hold your ax tightly, and strike it with another piece of wood. Never strike it with another ax.

To limb a tree start lopping the branches off at the bottom and work upward to the top. In this way you won't splinter the trunk.

With practice you will find that you will be able to carve and whittle with your hand ax too. Then it may even talk to you.

Each time a good camper picks up his ax he reminds himself that he is about to use a dangerous tool, that he cannot be too careful. Before he begins chopping he inspects the head of his ax to make sure it is secure, clears the area where he will cut, and makes sure that everyone is safely out of reach and out of the path of his swing. Then he goes to work.

It is not necessary for you to master all of the techniques of your logger cousins; but you should learn how to chop, cut, and hew with the two-handed ax. When you do you will feel more like a true woodsman.

First things first. Whether you wish to cut a standing tree or chop a down log, you must learn how to grip your ax and swing it properly. If you are right handed grasp the ax handle near its end with your left hand and near its head with your right. Raise the ax above your right shoulder and commence the swing from there, sliding your right hand back along the handle until it meets your left. This will accelerate the swing of the ax and add power to the blow.

Tackle a down log first. Protect yourself with a buffer log like the camper on the next page. It may save your leg or foot from a cut. Make your notch as wide as the log is thick. Cut half way through the log, then turn it and finish the job with another opposing or back notch. Remember these pointers.

When you prepare to fell a tree, clear the area so that you may cut a felling notch perpendicular to the line of fall you have chosen and a back notch on the other side. Cut the tree close to the ground unless you have a reason for leaving a high stump. Cut a deep felling notch as the camper has done on page 23 and a shallow back notch just a trifle higher. Then shout "timber-r-r" as she goes over on the hinge you left.

To hew a flat surface on that log make a series of slanting cuts on one side about three or four inches apart. Then start again and peel the loose chips from the log using a flat cutting or planing swing with your ax.

With some mastery of these basic techniques your ax will become a valuable tool and you a better camper.

HOW ABOUT A SAW?

Until the introduction of compact light-weight saws campers had little love for them, but now the wise camper would not be without one in the woods. A saw protected with a sheath is the safest cutting tool a camper can have, and it is a most useful one too. A saw will do many of the jobs an ax will, and do them quicker and better. As a provider of firewood it is unbeatable. A saw is useful in clearing deadfalls from the trail, in cutting logs for benches and other rustic furniture, and in cutting poles for shelter, rafts, and other things.

A number of excellent camp saws are available, both folding and rigid, but the two best are the small bow saw or "Swede Fiddle" pictured here and the camp saw with a blade which folds into its own wooden handle. The bow saw is light, compact, efficient, and a glutton for work. It is inexpensive and the best bet for the camper.

If you can afford a saw *or* an ax but not both, buy the saw first.

GIVE'R SNOOSE

As a camper you will seldom find it necessary to cut anything larger than a six-inch log. Your camp saw will meet the
challenge adequately if you follow a few simple rules and
"give'r a bit of snoose," as the old-timers would say.

When you cut firewood with your bow saw, as the campers are doing on the opposite page, remember to grasp the
frame firmly at the base near the blade, make long straight
strokes, and apply just a slight downward pressure. Keep the
blade straight. Do not twist it or it will pinch. Hold the piece
you are sawing at a safe distance from the cut, otherwise the
blade may jump from the kerf and cut your hand. Ask another
camper to hold the log you are cutting over a buck so that
you will have ample clearance and a steady log to saw. If
your blade binds ease it by applying a few drops of kerosene
or bacon grease.

When you decide to build that log cabin the same sawing
methods will hold, but you will need bigger tools such as the
cedar saw and peavy the campers are using in the illustration.

FLOATING ON AIR

Sleep—there is nothing like it for the weary camper. He can go without food, suffer sunburn and mosquitoes, and endure wet clothing; but he needs sleep, good comfortable sleep, each night.

Your forefathers were obliged to sleep on the ground in lumpy blanket rolls or buffalo robes. Sometimes they stuffed mattress ticks with dry leaves or fashioned beds of balsam boughs. But now—you may float on air. You may sleep on a light-weight inexpensive air mattress. Yes, for the camper, the air mattress is here to stay. Be sure you take one.

Air mattresses are available in many shapes, weights, and prices. The go-light camper should select a three-quarter length mattress of light vinyl weighing less than two pounds. The pack tripper or canoe cruiser should choose one of heavy plastic or rubberized nylon. In this day every camper should take an air mattress with him. Be sure you take one.

Caught without your mattress? Then manicure the ground you must sleep on. Remove every stone and pine cone and dig shallow holes for your hips and shoulders. If you must sleep on the ground make a contour bed of it first.

TRY A BAG

Blanket rolls and buffalo robes were fine for old woods-men but not for you. Invest instead in a sleeping bag and you will have many hours of sleeping comfort. A good bag will last for years and provide that rest which is so essential for the camper on the trail.

A light-weight bag is ideal for the average camper. Get one made of tough water-repellent poplin or of a synthetic material which is filled with down or a good grade of synthetic fiber carefully ribbed and quilted. Your bag should have a full length zipper so that it may be opened wide to the sun and air. Conditions under which the bag will be used will determine the weight of the fill. One and a half to two pounds of goose down is ample for a summer or fall bag. A winter one needs more. Once you use a good sleeping bag and air mattress like the campers shown here you will never be caught without them on the trail.

Learn to roll your bag tightly, very tightly like the camper in the picture on the opposite page. Fold it lengthwise; then start to roll it and keep a steady pressure on it with your knee. Result—a small compact bag which is easy to pack. Fold your air mattress. Do not roll it.

29

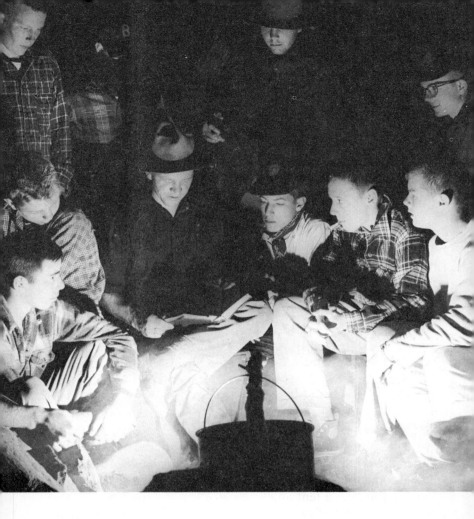

AT NIGHT BY THE FIRE

Night and the magic of the campfire—that same magic which has captured the imagination of men since time began. You will feel it when you sit by the fire, when you gaze into the flames, when you listen to stories of the plainsmen and the voyageurs. And in the black night which surrounds you the grotesque shadows and weird noises will push you ever closer to the warmth and friendship which is the fire.

YOU CAN TAKE IT WITH YOU

Unlike your frontier ancestors who were obliged to rough it with a set of buckskins, a rifle, a bit of parched corn, some pemmican, and a blanket, and to live off the land, you can "take it with you." You can take all the food, clothing, and equipment you need to camp in comfort whether you go by boat, bicycle, car, canoe, horse, or on foot and be your own pack mule. The secret is in knowing what to have and how to carry it.

If you take to the trail on foot like the go-light camper on page 33, you should keep your load to an absolute minimum. Take only those items which are essential. Unless you plan to venture into deep wilderness a small supply of food will do, and you may replenish this along the way. You will need a pack sack. One of the least expensive and most practical is the haversack made famous by the scouts. For more comfort and more capacity select a rucksack or frame pack such as the one used by the camper in the picture. This is an excellent pack, useful for many types of camping.

Learn to pack your sack correctly and adjust your pack straps so they fit you. The pack should ride high and snug, not hang down on your back. As a hiker you will need a lightweight sleeping bag and air mattress, one change of clothes, a skillet, pot, plate, pannikin, cup, fork and spoon, a pocketknife, towel and toilet articles, matches, some first-aid supplies, food, a bit of money, a tarp or poncho, and a rain parka. Even if you take a tent and a few extra frills your load should not exceed twenty-five pounds unless you are a husky person.

If you plan to travel by canoe or boat where some portaging will be involved, you may need more food and more equipment such as saws and axes, shoes and fishing tackle. Then you will want a Duluth Pack to tote that bigger load. If you go by car there is little limit to what you may take, and duffle bags will prove most appropriate. Many auto campers carry portable stoves, collapsible tubs, folding chairs, and ice chests—and why not! Where weight is no deterrent let comfort and convenience be your guide.

IN BAGS, BAGS, BAGS

Even the earliest campers used bags, skin bags with no fancy straps, but bags they were and bags they have remained, for bags are still a camper's best means of sorting, storing, and transporting his food, clothing, and equipment.

Modern plastic and rubberized bags have been a real boon to the camper. They are tough, inexpensive, lightweight, and waterproof, and the experienced camper is using more bags than ever.

Collect a good supply of bags before you pack for a trip: some tough plastic ones in assorted sizes, some cotton bags with tie strings, a few small rubberized ones, and one or two large bags for those bulky items. Pack your sleeping bag in a large bag, your spare clothing in another, your toilet articles in one plastic bag, your soap in a plastic box and that with your towel in another bag. Pack extra shoes in a rubberized bag, film and writing materials in a plastic bag, and your shirts and sweat suit in another. Pack dry foods in individual plastic bags, pack these in cotton bags, and your cook kit in a canvas bag. Then load all of these bags into one large rubberized bag and put that one in your packsack. Tuck your rain parka on top, and you are ready to go.

OR BASKETS

Baskets for campers? Yes, baskets! For centuries Indians and trappers of the north have carried pack baskets along with their bags and sacks. The Adirondack or Maine pack basket is still used widely because of its light weight, rigid shape, durability, and convenience. If you have an opportunity, give one of these white ash baskets a trial. You may find it all to your liking.

The pack basket has been favored by many hikers because it rides comfortably on the back, is easy to pack and suitable for the transport of bulky items such as canned goods, tools, and fishing tackle which, in a packsack, would gouge the back of the hiker unmercifully. It has been used by trappers to carry their traps, animals, and furs. Picnickers and overnighters like it because their sandwiches and potato chips come through without being smashed. Old-timers use it because it has the old-time flavor and tradition of the woods.

OR WANNIGANS

For the pack tripper, canoe cruiser, or auto camper no pack is more practical than the pannier, wannigan, or tote box, that rugged box designed specifically to carry cooking utensils, canned food, and bulky or breakable items. In its original form this "jewel box" was a heavy wooden affair often covered with rawhide. Today the best ones are made of light wood, fiber, plastic, or a combination of these materials.

Good panniers measure about 20 by 20 by 12 inches. They are used in pairs and attached to a pack saddle by means of leather loops. Tote boxes for auto campers may be designed to fit individual needs, but they should be sound and sturdy.

The canoe cruiser's wannigan pictured here measures 24 by 12 by 14 inches. All joints are carefully screwed together and doubly reinforced with waterproof glue. The lid for this one is attached with bent-nail catches, but some are fastened with suitcase-type pull down latches and waterproofed with a bit of rubber gasket.

The wannigan is an ideal pack for portaging heavy loads over short distances. It is carried with a leather strap known as a tumpline or with shoulder straps and a tump strap which are attached. As you see, an extra pack or duffle may be carried on top.

You will like the versatile wannigan. It is not only an excellent pack for carrying, but also a handy pantry, work-table, and bench in the camp kitchen.

YOU WILL WANT A TENT

There are sections of the plains and places in the mountains where rain is sparse and insects almost unheard of where you may camp in complete comfort without tent or shelter. But these areas are exceptions. There are circumstances where the weight factor may prevent you from carrying a tent, but when you camp in the woods you will be exposed to weather and insects and you will want a tent. If it is possible you should have one. Select a tent which is suited to your needs and your budget.

Tents today are made from a multitude of materials and in many shapes and sizes. The variety of tents seems endless and you must choose wisely.

What are the features of a good tent? A good one is carefully made of strong light-weight material, such as fine cotton which has been treated with a water-repellent or water-proof substance. Unfortunately, the lighter and stronger the material is the more expensive the tent will be. A good tent must be tough for it will take a beating. It should have ample reinforcement at the points of stress, such as the corners, tie tapes, ridges, pole holes, and grommets. It should have a sewn-in floor made of a tough waterproof material, such as neoprene-impregnated nylon. It should have sewn-in netting which may be opened with zippers or snaps or both. It should be easy to pitch and easy to pack. It should be bug proof, snake proof, and vermin proof.

Most of the so-called one-man tents are quite impractical. They are too cramped and too expensive for the protection they afford. Besides, who wants to be a hermit camper? For beginners the two-man pup tent with sewn-in floor and netting like the one illustrated on the preceding page is ideal. If you expect to have three campers in your group, a modified explorer's tent like the one pictured on this page, or one of the modern three-man pop-up tents may be just what you want. It will afford more headroom than the pup tent, and headroom is a valuable asset in a tent.

If you plan to camp with a party of five or six, you may use two of the three-man tents or invest in a six-man cruising model, such as the baker tent shown on this page. This is an excellent all-weather tent which provides a maximum of protection and comfort for a minimum of bulk and weight. It has ample room for the occupants to stand. In winter a reflector fire in front of this baker tent will keep its occupants warm and cozy.

The recently introduced suspension tents which are supported by an external framework of sectional poles are superb. They are expensive but worth every cent to the camper who is contemplating an expedition into remote territory, the mountains or the barren grounds. They have their own poles. They need no pegs.

Going by auto? Then the big umbrella tent is the one for you. It is roomy and comfortable, and most are made of good watertight materials. Many have awnings, zipper windows, and extra screens.

When you camp, camp in comfort—camp in a tent.

PITCH IT

The best tent may be damaged quickly by careless treatment, and it may provide miserable shelter if improperly set on a poor site. From the outset learn to handle your tent with the utmost care and to pitch it properly in a well-chosen spot.

Select a location away from trees which may blow over or drop dead limbs on you in a storm. Pick one on a knoll if you can, one high enough to drain well and be safe from flash floods. Pick a spot away from swamps, tall grass, and brush which may harbor insects; pick a spot away from sandy beaches, one which is shaded and protected by trees but open to gentle breezes. Face your tent away from the threat of wind and rain, otherwise face it to the east so the rising sun will dry it and wake you in time for an early start on the trail.

Like the campers in the picture here stretch the floor of your tent flat and peg it down first. With the floor securely fastened, raise the ridge to the proper height, hold it in the correct position, and set your poles as the campers have done in the picture on the next page. Then you are ready to secure the various guy lines which will give your tent shape and strength.

TENT MAGIC

There are tricks in the camper's bag of tent magic which you should know before you hit the trail, or you may be forced to learn them the hard way later on. First, learn to tie a bowline and throw a clove hitch. Use that bowline whenever you need a loop in a rope, the clove hitch when you secure ropes to poles, sticks, or pegs.

When you pitch your tent stretch it tightly; but when rain threatens loosen the ridge and guy ropes a trifle for a wet tent shrinks, and it may shrink enough to rip or pull its own pegs and collapse. Be careful not to touch the top of your tent in the rain unless you want a shower. Your touch will temporarily destroy the surface tension which makes your tent shed water.

Before you strike a tent clean it thoroughly inside and out. Sticks and pebbles inside may punch holes when you roll it. Be sure your tent is dry before you pack it, for a wet tent will mildew and rot. To produce a compact tent fold it into a long narrow bundle, begin to roll it and apply constant pressure to the roll with your knee like the campers in the picture. If you roll pegs with your tent be sure to wrap them in a piece of old blanket or cloth first, otherwise they may punch holes in it.

SHELTER HELTER SKELTER

If you are a hiker or go-light camper you may be obliged to challenge the great outdoors without the comfort of a tent, and in this case bad weather will force you to rely upon your woodcraft skill and wits for shelter. Even if you camp with a tent it may be lost or destroyed, and you should know how to provide emergency shelter of some type.

Caves are few and far between. It is pure luck if you find a nice dry one. But if you carry a poncho or tarp and a bit of line you may do quite well. Your best bet is a poncho den such as the one the camper has made in the picture here. Two campers with ponchos may fasten them together and come up with something resembling a pup tent. If you have a canoe, turn it on its side, anchor one edge of your poncho to it and the other to the ground, and crawl under.

If you are trapped without a poncho or tarp, look for a large hollow tree, or a bunker or overhanging ledge which may shield you from the rain; or make a brush den by leaning some poles against a large down log and covering them with limbs from evergreens or with any type of leafy boughs. You will be amazed at the amount of water shed by a den of this type.

THAT TARP

Because of its bulk and weight the old-fashioned canvas tarpaulin was considered a useless burden by many campers. The advent of plastics and plastic-filled fabrics made extremely light, compact tarps available, and most campers have learned to appreciate the value of this versatile camp item. An ideal tarp measures about six by eight feet and has a dozen or more grommets evenly spaced in its well-hemmed edges.

The primary function of a tarp is the protection of food and equipment by day and firewood at night. That first rainy morning in the woods will show you the wisdom of this precaution.

If you travel by canoe, that tarp and a bit of nylon line you should have to use with it will make an excellent sail when winds are favorable. At the campsite it will make a fly under which you may cook and eat in the rain or cool yourself in the sun. A tarp may be used as a ground cloth, an extra blanket, a wind screen, a snow fly, or a water bag. In an emergency an adequate stretcher can be fashioned from a tarp and a few poles. Sooner or later a tarp should and will find its way into your modern camping outfit.

YOUR COOK KIT

To paraphrase an old army expression, a camper travels on his stomach. To maintain his health and morale he must have well-prepared food in ample quantity. Many old-time campers pride themselves on their cooking genius, and all they ask to produce a culinary miracle is a variety of basic camp foods and a topnotch cook kit.

Some day the label of camp cook extraordinary may be attached to you, and when that time arrives you undoubtedly will have a fine cook kit of your own. To begin with you should acquire two or three small nesting pots, a steel skillet, some plastic or aluminum plates and bowls, some plastic or steel cups, and forks, spoons, spatulas and can opener.

The heart of a good cook kit lies in a nest of pots with bail handles and lids. Most camp foods are boiled, broiled, steamed, warmed, or baked. Some are fried, but these are in the minority.

Unfortunately the popular scout and army mess kits are in reality not cook kits at all; they are merely eating kits. It is almost impossible for a good cook to produce anything better than scorched bacon and scrambled eggs or burned hamburger and cocoa in one of these. The challenge may be intriguing, but the results hardly worth it.

Unless you are a hermit you may anticipate cooking for a minimum of two campers and a maximum of many more. You will do well to develop a cook kit somewhat similar to that which the campers are using on the page opposite. It contains a nest of five aluminum pots fitted with bail handles and lids, two round steel skillets with folding handles, a collapsible aluminum reflector oven with two baking pans, two aluminum plates and a nest of plastic plates, a nest of plastic bowls, a nest of plastic cups, one cooking fork, two large steel cooking spoons, one pancake turner, two small can openers, stainless table forks and tea spoons, a spatula, two table knives, and a pair of gloves. You may wish to add some frills to yours, but this basic outfit is adequate to whip up many a tasty camp meal.

READY, SET, GO

Once you have studied the equipment requirements of a camper and purchased a few of the necessary items you are ready to begin camping. But where? Strange as it seems your own back yard may provide the best practice field. There you may pitch your tent and strike it; practice this until you can do it quickly and successfully even under adverse conditions.

Bring in a few dead trees or logs and practice your axmanship and sawmanship. Then practice packing your tent, clothing, and equipment in your pack sack, and toting the loaded pack for a while. You may find that your straps are too long or that a pot is gouging your back. Repack your sack, readjust it, and try again.

Build a small fireplace like the camper on the next page and try cooking a few simple foods. Better to suffer cooking disasters near home where you may run to the pantry for reserves than on the trail where you may go hungry. When you are through practicing, strike camp and clean your "campsite" thoroughly. This is just one mark of a good camper.

Now try a trip to one of your city or county parks or to some outlying woods where camping is permitted. The hike to a local campground and a weekend of camping there will tell you much about your outfit and your ability. You may find that your shoes do not fit as well as they must, that you need a few additional items of equipment, or that you can do without some of those you have.

After a number of trips to local spots you should be ready for an expedition to some of the wonderful state and national parks which dot our country from coast to coast. This experience will help develop your camping skill and can only whet your appetite for the challenge and adventure of real camping in the vast open spaces of the west, the mountains, or the great forests of the north. Every true camper looks forward to the time when he may head into the wilderness,

living and traveling and surviving on his very own. If he is prepared with good equipment and some degree of skill, this wilderness adventure will provide all of the fun and challenge he has hoped for. If he lacks camping know-how, misery and disaster may be his only reward.

BUT HOW

Not too many years ago camping was a way of life for many Americans. It was their profession, and in spite of the hardships involved they loved it. There were but three ways to travel, three we still use today: on foot, by horse, by canoe. A choice of means was simplified by the economic facts of life—if you had a horse or a canoe you used it, if not you went on foot.

Today your method of travel depends not only on your budget, but also on the trip you plan. If your route parallels the highways you should go by car if you can afford it, otherwise by foot. If you expect to leave the highway you must go by foot, by horse, or by canoe like the old-timers, or by plane, perhaps, if your bank account can stand the strain. Each of these methods of camping has its attractive features and its drawbacks, and you should consider them all before you go.

Travel by foot and you make contact with the great outdoors in all its natural splendor. You will develop strong legs and sound endurance, but you may sleep wet on some occasions.

Travel by auto and you see the broad panorama of the country spread out before you. You leap from one point of interest to another, but you do not build a keen eye, a strong arm, and a straight back.

Travel by horse and you gain the feel of the open spaces, of the mountains and all their scenic grandeur. The air is pungent with smoke and herd dust, but you must wrangle those horses, feed and water them.

Travel by plane and you reach your destination in a painless twinkling. You jump over the vast wilderness, the mountains and forests. You land at a secluded lake where fish wait to be caught, but you lose the challenge and adventure of real camping, of meeting the elements head on.

Travel by canoe and you travel like the voyageurs of old. You toil with paddle and pack through remote regions where moose splashing in the marsh and ducks flying overhead may distract you from your work. It is hard work, and your body will grow tough and supple with each day's travel; but you miss much in the way of wildlife that does not come down to the water to drink.

BY COMPASS AND MAP

The first time roads end and marked trails vanish and you must find your way by map and compass, you will feel either the exhilirating thrill of exploration or the bottomless despair of being lost. So a bit of practice with map and compass in known territory is a sensible precaution.

The ideal compass for the camper is a small durable pocket model, such as the one pictured, or a wrist compass or a lensatic model with plastic base. With one of these, a good set of maps, and a bit of know-how, you should be able to find your way through any wilderness area remaining in North America.

Good maps are essential, and they are available in the United States from the Map Information Office, U.S. Geological Survey, Washington 25, D.C., and in Canada from the Map Distribution Office, Department of Mines and Technical Surveys, Ottawa, Canada.

The primary problem for the beginner in navigating by map and compass is one of visualization. You must learn to orient your map with the actual terrain and associate visual landmarks with those shown on the map. To do this place your

compass over your present location on your map, and turn both map and compass until the compass needle points to magnetic north on the compass rose and the north-south lines on the map are parallel with the north-south lines of your compass. This done you will have your map oriented like the camper in the picture. If your map shows some significant land feature near your present location, look in the direction indicated by the map and see if the feature is actually there. If it is you know two things: that you are where you thought you were, that your map is properly oriented.

Now check the direction you wish to travel on your map, and look in that same direction for some landmark which may serve as a guidepost for you. Proceed to this new landmark, and when you reach it check the accuracy of your position again. By repeating this simple process you will be able to check your position at all times and proceed in a chosen direction.

One sad note—all maps are not absolutely accurate. Don't be flustered when an island turns up out of nowhere. Just report this fact to the Map Information Office. They will thank you for your trouble.

CAMP IS WHERE YOU FIND IT

Selecting a campsite is just a matter of choosing a comfortable spot in one of the well-defined, carefully designated areas when you camp in city, state or national parks; it can also be quite a challenge when you venture into the forest or the wilderness beyond. Good campsites, as you will quickly discover, are often few and far between. Unless he is aiming for a specific campsite the wise old-timer starts looking for one in the early afternoon. He does not relish the thought of being trapped on the move by darkness. He enjoys making camp early so that he will have time to hike through the surrounding countryside, study the wildlife, and go fishing or swimming before he prepares that tasty evening meal.

What should you look for in a good campsite? An ideal one has three main features: relatively high ground safe from floods with enough space for tents and a good kitchen, ready access to pure water in quantity, and an ample supply of good firewood. Sites meeting these requirements are plentiful in

some areas, almost non-existent in others. In the mountains you may have a tough time finding a good level spot, and wood may be scarce. On the plains water is sometimes a problem, and a canteen may be your only source. Search for a good campsite, but remember that when darkness begins to close in camp is where you find it.

In the picture on page 52 the campers have just arrived at a good site and begun to unload their canoes. In the picture above they are organizing their camp community. Tents will be pitched on ground which is fairly level, free of rocks and stumps. The camp kitchen will be established near the lake where a fireplace may be built on bed rock and protected somewhat from the wind. The swimming area looks inviting, but a number of campers will wade through it to detect any submerged rocks or other obstacles before anyone dives into the water.

A good camp evening seems to be in the making for this group.

IT NEEDS A FIREPLACE

The heart of any campsite is its fireplace. It should be a good one, for if anything is indispensable to camping it is the warmth and friendship of fire, fire which heats tents and dries clothes, fire which casts flickering shadows in the trees at night, fire which cooks food in a pot.

The best material from which to build a fireplace is rock, and rocks are available in most areas, but not all. Green logs are second on the list, followed in order by sod, clay and a hole in the ground. A good rock fireplace should be large enough to accommodate three or four pots and a reflector oven. It should consist of a back, or reflector wall two or three feet long and 12 to 18 inches high, and two wing walls 18 inches long and 6 to 12 inches high. Before you begin to build, assemble a large pile of rocks and select the flattest and largest for your reflecting surface. The back wall should be sturdy enough to support waugan sticks (holders) for pots, and flat enough to throw heat into a reflector oven. Try to fit the rocks together carefully like these campers so that a sturdy fireplace will result.

After the large rocks are in place chink crevices and brace wobbly corners with small ones. If possible, build flat tops on the wing walls so you may set cooking utensils on them and keep pots warms.

When rocks are not available the best cooking rig is the famous hunter-trapper fireplace of the woods in the picture above. It is made from two green logs, five to eight inches in diameter and two to three feet long, which are placed one beside the other. They are close enough at one end to support a small pot and at the other to support a skillet. A fire is laid between these logs. A damper stick placed under one end of the windward log will raise it enough to permit the circulation of air and a draft for the fire.

When no rocks or green trees are available cut squares of sod or chunks of hard clay and stack these in the form of a fireplace, or dig a trench-like hole in the ground just wide enough to support your pots. These methods are difficult but workable.

If you have the misfortune to camp in a location where open fires are prohibited, you will find it necessary to cook on some type of portable stove fueled with gasoline, kerosene, bottled gas or alcohol, and you will miss the romance and mystery of a camp fire.

A RUSTIC KITCHEN LAYOUT

A well-organized kitchen is a must for the busy camp cook who should have everything at hand when and where he needs it. Use the camp fireplace as a cornerstone and build the balance of the layout around it.

Careful control of fire is the first essential of skillful camp cooking and an ample supply of good firewood is necessary to assure this control. The cook should never want for wood. It should be cut and stacked carefully at one side of the fireplace where it is within easy reach. The other side of the fireplace should be a location for a work surface or a storage area for packs and equipment.

If you carry a number of packs or wannigans arrange them in similar order each time you establish a new kitchen. This will save searching and confusion. Place your packs in a row with the tin (kitchen) pack nearest the fireplace, like the campers above. This arrangement will permit the cook to take something from any pack without stepping over others. The camp kitchen also serves as headquarters for axes, saws, tarps and the first-aid kit.

For protection all these items should be stored between packs and returned to their same location after each use. If this is done you will not only know where to find them, but also know that, when missing, they are in use.

The cook will need a work surface: a place to slice meat, roll the pie dough and mix puddings, a place to set pots and utensils, a place to organize food. Wannigan tops make an excellent work surface, as does the bottom of a canoe which has been braced on a pair of logs like the one below. If you have time to build it, a rustic table will work out well. In a pinch a board or clean flat rock will suffice. At meal time this work surface may be converted into a cafeteria counter: a place to set plates, cups, forks, and the food to be served.

If you plan to bake, place the reflector oven in front of the fire and level it. With a small amount of water in the pan prop the corners and legs with small pieces of flat stone or chips of wood until the water stands evenly. It must be level to work properly.

One law of the woods you should know and observe: stay out of the kitchen unless you are a cook. Fewer people there means less chance that dirt will be kicked in the food or pots upset.

AND SOME RUSTIC FURNISHINGS

Learn to improve each campsite with the few rustic furnishings which time may permit you to make, and you will learn to "smooth it" rather than rough it.

If you have a rock fireplace waugan sticks are a must. They are made from trimmed saplings, preferably green, which are from 6 to 12 feet long and about one inch in diameter at the small end. Anchor the butt of each sapling on the ground with a rock or log so that its tip will extend over the back of your fireplace and support one or two pots over the fire. To adjust pots raise the stick with wedge, or move the butt, or both. When you use a waugan stick remember to take it down before you break camp. It's bad luck to leave that waugan standing in the woods.

With a hunter-trapper fireplace your best bet for pot support is a camp crane or Chippewa Kitchen. The crane is made by cutting two sturdy forked sticks about 30 inches long and driving one into the ground at each end of the fireplace. Lay a pole in the forks and suspend pots over the fire with pot hooks fashioned from small forked sticks which have notches cut in them to hold the pot bails as in the picture on page 58.

Rustic benches are desirable and are most easily fashioned from large dead trees. If a tree with a diameter of 6 to 12 inches is available cut a few sections about four feet long and hew a flat surface on one side of each. Support these on stones or other pieces of log which have been notched to prevent the big ones from rolling. A triangular rustic table can be constructed readily if you have a bit of binder twine and utilize standing trees for at least two legs. Lash one stick across the trees at table height and two more sticks, one to each tree and to a third stick or leg, at the same height. Then lay other sticks and limbs across this triangular support to form a rustic table surface.

When camped away from lakes or streams a rustic wash

stand and towel rack like that in the picture may be advisable. It will discourage your fellow campers from washing their hands in your kitchen pots. These are but a few of the furnishings you can contrive from materials in the woods. The good camper prides himself on his ingenuity and takes time to make himself comfortable and happy.

AND FIRE

What is a camper's best friend? Fire, of course! It is indispensable to his comfort on the trail, and every accomplished camper learns all he can about the art of firebuilding. He takes pride in his ability to make many kinds of fires from all types of materials under varying conditions. He is apt to laugh at the tenderfoot who struggles to build a fire with a few chunks of punky wood, a wad of leaves and a handful of matches.

In some ways firebuilding may be likened to homebuilding. You must know the materials required, gather an adequate supply and put them together properly to produce a good fire. Four things are needed: a starter, some tinder, kindling and firewood.

The right starter for the modern camper is a wooden match. Oh, you can start a fire like the old-time Indians by rubbing two sticks together or striking flint on steel but these

methods are parade ground stunts now and quite impractical for regular camping. You need matches, and it is wise to take twice as many as you think you will require.

Protect your general supply by packing it in a friction top tin or a waterproof bag, and always carry an emergency supply in your pocket in a waterproof match safe.

Dry paper makes excellent tinder, but the woodsman prefers native tinder for his fires and birch bark is best, bar none. It will burn fiercely, wet or dry. Do not cut birch bark from a live tree; just pull off a few loose curls, or cut some bark from a dead tree. A handful of bark peeled into thin sheets is ample. When birch bark is not available, shredded cedar bark, shaving clusters or twig tinder will do nicely.

Make a shaving cluster by whittling a group of long thin shavings from a piece of very dry soft wood such as pine or cedar. Do not cut the shavings free of the piece one at a time but in clusters of four or five like those on page 60. Five or six of these clusters are sufficient to start almost any fire.

Twig tinder consists of a bunch of the driest tiniest dead twigs you can gather from the branches of standing trees. These must snap with a sharp "crack" when you break them. A fistful of twigs no bigger than a soda straw should be sufficient.

The selection of kindling and firewood is apt to separate the true camper from the tenderfoot because a knowledge of

trees and wood is absolutely essential for success. An experienced camper can identify many common trees in summer and winter. He knows that softwoods make the best kindling and hardwoods the best firewood; that in general all evergreen trees are soft and all broadleaf trees hard, that there are exceptions such as basswood, elder and tulip which are soft and fir which may seem hard.

Softwoods make wonderful kindling because they light easily and burn fiercely; they fairly explode with heat, but they do not burn long. Squaw wood, the dry branches you may break from standing trees, makes good kindling, but finely split cedar is better. It burns with a hot crackling flame. It gives wonderful light. If cedar is available select it first and basswood or pine second. When you lay a fire be sure to use an ample supply of kindling or you may be obliged to lay it a second time.

Hardwoods make good firewood because they burn slowly and evenly and have lasting power. The best among the hardwoods are white oak, maple, hickory, birch and beech. All leave a wonderful bed of coals. Good firewood is made from branches or logs which have been sawed into lengths and split or quartered. Remember, split wood always burns better.

A few trees including aspen, cottonwood and willow may be used for kindling or firewood. They have some properties of both, but the best of neither. Ash is unique becaues it will burn when green.

After you have assembled all of these materials begin to lay your fire and be sure to start with the old-fashioned tepee or wigwam, for this is not only a fire in itself but a core for most other fires. Bunch your tinder and place it on a dry spot in the center of the fireplace. Then starting with the smallest, place sticks of kindling over your tinder in tepee fashion, and keep adding sticks until you come up with a wigwam like the one in the picture on page 62. It should burn well, for a fire needs fuel, heat, and oxygen to burn, and this wigwam will give it the best of all.

CRISS CROSS FOR COOKING

With just a bit of replenishing that wigwam fire alone will prove quite adequate to simmer a kettle of soup or cook a simple one-pot meal, for it supplies concentrated heat quickly. You should use it, for a good camper uses the smallest fire possible. When you tackle a dinner which includes foods that must be boiled, broiled, fried or baked you will need a larger more lasting fire, and you must add some hardwood to your wigwam; add it in the form of a crude log cabin like that pictured here. You will have the famous criss-cross fire of the woodsman, a wonderful fire for cooking because it burns quickly and evenly and makes a good bed of coals.

Before you light this fire stand your reflector oven in front of the fireplace where it will catch the hot blast of the flames and bake your pies, cakes and meats. Hang pots over the fire to boil water for soup and tea, and as long as you need flame and high heat for boiling and baking replenish your fire frequently; keep the wood stacked high. When the baking is done and you wish to fry or broil, flatten the fire to a bed of coals.

INDIAN FOR LIGHT AND WARMTH

Fire is not only a means of cooking, but a source of heat and light for the camper who ventures forth on those short cold days in late fall or winter. Like the old-time Indian he should know how to build crackling council fires of split soft wood which spit and spark as they light up a lodge or campsite, lazy-man fires of whole logs on rollers which glow with a steady warmth, and reflector fires which make a tent cozy.

No one relishes the idea of pulling on a set of cold clammy clothes on a frosty morning. The experienced camper guards against such an unpleasant possibility by building a reflector fire, like the one here, a yard or so in front of his tent where it will not scorch the canvas. The reflector he makes of stone, or green logs stacked against two sticks driven at a slight angle. He lays a large tepee fire against it so the smoke will draw up and away. Before he goes to sleep he lights the fire and then replenishes it during the night, or he makes a mad dash to light it in the morning, crawls back in his sleeping bag and waits for his tent to warm and become toasty before he climbs out to dress and tackle the morning work.

GOOD FOOD AND PLENTY OF IT

Camping is hard work. It burns up calories in great quantities. Ravenous appetites are standard equipment for most campers everywhere, and well-balanced appetizing meals are essential to maintain the morale of any group. The primary factors which govern the type and variety of food a camper should have are the type of trip he will take and the method of travel he will employ.

The auto camper who is always within easy reach of a grocery store finds his menu limited only by his imagination and the condition of his wallet. He may dine like a gourmet if money and his culinary talents permit. He may include fresh fruits, vegetables and meats just as he would at home, and these are foods his counterpart in the backwoods must do without.

The camper who leaves the highway relishes a variety of well prepared food like his auto-camping cousin, but he must carry all of the food for his trip and he realizes that weight, bulk and a lack of refrigeration are limiting factors. Before he departs he must carefully consider the length of his trip, the conditions he will encounter, his means of travel, the equipment he will have, and the possibility of resupplying en route. Then he must plan a menu to fit the situation. If he is going for any length of time he must select foods which will provide the greatest nutritional value for the least amount of weight, and he must take pains to protect all of his food from weather, loss or spoilage.

The wise camper packs much of his food in tough plastic bags like those you see on page 67. Some he takes in cloth bags, some in plastic bottles, some in cartons and cans, none in glass. No matter how small his food list may be he is careful to include a few items which will add taste, variety and vitamins to the basic menu. Those frills are essential for happy eating.

For the sake of organization the experienced camper usually considers food in five or six separate categories when

planning his menu. These include staples, meats, dairy products, fruits and vegetables, cereals, and beverages. The staples on his food list include such well-known items as salt, black pepper, cinnamon, white and brown sugar; condiments including mustard, catsup and tomato paste; dehydrated soups, cooking oil, and calorie-rich foods like peanut butter, jam, syrup base and candy bars.

Although fresh meats must be ruled out for lack of refrigeration an amazing variety of dried, canned, smoked and spiced meats may be used and all are loaded with flavor and energy. Those you see on page 69—side bacon, back bacon, summer sausage, dried beef and corned beef—form the backbone of any camper's meat list; but canned or smoked ham, meat balls, pork loaf, Spam, chicken, bologna and sausage are good also. All of these meats provide excellent protein food value and a quantity of animal fats which are most essential.

Recent developments have brought a number of dehydrated and flash-frozen dehydrated meats to the market. These hold great promise for the future. Those now available are packaged for the most part with other ingredients to form hashes, stews and casseroles. A number of processors sell packages designed especially for trip use which will serve two, four or six people.

Dairy items have a most important place on the camp food list because of the energy-giving proteins and bone-building minerals they contain. Eggs, butter, cheese and powdered milk, on page 69, are all useful in a variety of ways. Cheese may be eaten plain or in sandwiches or blended with other foods. Powdered milk may be consumed as a beverage, but its primary use is in cocoa, potatoes, puddings and other dishes. By themselves powdered eggs are a bad risk, but they are useful in batters and for baking. Whole eggs can and should be carried for their variety value.

No true woodsman would ever venture forth without tea. Tea is the camper's beverage par excellence. A little goes a long way, and whether the temperature is nine or ninety

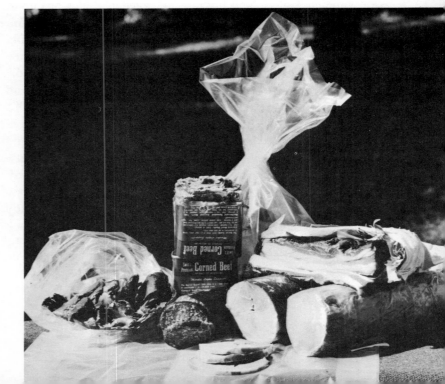

nothing will provide stimulus and comfort better than a cup of hot tea in the late afternoon. A bit of instant coffee is fine for flavor, but it lacks food value, and the active camper prefers cocoa for breakfast. It's loaded!

For a noon-time refresher or before-dinner "cocktail" try a bit of pink lemonade. That sweet-sour flavor is most refreshing and the sugar provides extra energy. Younger campers in particular appreciate lemonade. Dehydrated orange juice and concentrated orange juice, both available, are highly recommended as breakfast beverages because of the vitamins they contain and the flavor and the variety they add.

Only a few fresh vegetables will survive camping conditions for long. All contain so much water that they are worthy of consideration only as delicacies, but it is wonderful to munch on a few carrot sticks or some slaw after a week or more in the bush. In spite of the weight of a few cans of vegetables the prudent camper may carry them because of their variety value, but the camper who wants vegetables with his meals should carry most of them in dehydrated form. Good ones include carrots, cabbage, turnips, green beans, sweet corn, spinach, onions and potatoes in powder, flakes or cubes. Instant potatoes and rice are tops for camp meals. Be sure you have plenty. Flash-frozen dehydrated vegetables are becoming available and they will prove quite a boon for campers. They cook quickly, yet retain all of their natural flavor and color.

Fruits are essential for the vitamins they supply, and while fresh fruits are impractical to take, dried fruits make a wonderful contribution to the food list. They weigh little, require little space. They are delicious when stewed and good to nibble on dry. They can be used in pies, cobblers and shortcakes. They go a long way toward livening an otherwise drab menu. Those pictured: apricots, raisins and prunes are among the best; pears, apples and peaches are also excellent. Many of these fruits now are available in a tasty low moisture pack rather than the pure dry pack. Whichever pack you select be sure to take an ample supply.

Breads and cereals are the staff of life for the camper as

they are for everyone, and the bulk of your bakery pack should be made up of mixes like those pictured: cake mix, biscuit mix, pancake mix, pudding mix, roll mix and pie crust mix. These are available in a multitude of brands and variations most of which are excellent.

Oats and Cream of Wheat head the list of cereals. In a broad sense this includes spaghetti and macaroni, two fine camp items. Bread itself may be carried for a considerable period when freshly baked and double wrapped, and pilot crackers will keep indefinitely when protected by a waterproof package.

Once you are familiar with the available supplies you may assume the role of maitre d'campsite, plan your menus and order food.

If everything must travel on your back variety will be limited, but big breakfasts, skimpy lunches and huge dinners are traditional for working campers, including hikers.

If you expect to travel by horse or canoe you should be able to tote more grub and expand your menus accordingly. A good camp breakfast may include juice, hot cereal with dried fruit, milk and brown sugar, pancakes, back bacon and cocoa. The skimpy lunch may consist of meat, cheese or peanut butter and jelly sandwiches, hot soup and candy bars. The sumptious dinner should feature lemonade, meat, a starch, a vegetable, tea and luscious dessert such as pie or cake.

Every old line camp cook collects prize recipes. Perhaps you will find these worthy of consideration.

Canadian Wonders: Cut a piece of back bacon into slices a third of an inch thick; brown both sides of each slice in a skillet; add enough fruit juice and fruit to cover the slices and simmer over low heat for about fifteen minutes. Add a pinch of powdered coffee, stir and serve. About two slices per person.

Corned Beef-n-Cheese: For five people empty two cans of corned beef into a pot; add about one-third can of sharp cheddar cheese cut into cubes, a liberal pinch of onion flakes and one-third can of water. Simmer over a slow fire stirring constantly until beef-n-cheese are piping hot. Serve plain, on biscuits, or over mashed potatoes.

Strawberry Tarts: Cut a thinly rolled piece of pie crust into six-inch squares; moisten the edges of each square with water; place a generous spoonful of strawberry preserves in the middle of each and fold into a triangular sandwich. Crimp the edges with a fork and bake in a reflector oven until they are golden brown and drooly.

Some Mores: Toast a marshmallow slowly over coals until well browned, then squeeze it between two chocolate graham crackers and devour. You will want some more!

Kabobs: On a green stick skewer the end of a slice of bacon, a chunk of round steak and the bacon again, a piece of onion and the bacon, another piece of steak and the bacon, a piece of cheese and the bacon, another piece of steak and the bacon. Roast slowly and thoroughly over a bed of coals. Serve on a bun.

FOOD FOOD EVERYWHERE

Although a prudent camper plans every phase of an expedition from departure to return with the utmost care, he must always recognize the possibility of disaster; the chance that he may find himself in the wilderness with little or no food or equipment. Should this happen his survival will depend upon woodcraft skill and a knowledge of the many natural foods which exist in the area.

In reality a camper is surrounded by food in almost any situation unless he happens to be on the top of a mountain peak. He also carries quite a reserve of food in his generally over-nourished body, and he can survive for quite a period on water alone, but that is no reason for him to fight the pangs of hunger.

If a camper manages to salvage his survival kit containing a few hooks and some line he can fish for his dinner in lake and stream country or set snares for rabbits and other small animals in the woods or prairies. If he has some mosquito netting he may be able to capture a few pounds of minnows, which are particularly nourishing when eaten whole whether cooked or raw. In general he may eat almost any creature he is able to capture whether it walks, crawls, slithers, flies or swims. The trick is in the catching.

In the woods the porcupine is considered the number one survival animal and a true woodsman never kills one except in case of emergency. Mr. Porky is slow and clumsy, easily killed with a club. Field mice also are readily captured in heavy grass. Turtles, snakes and lizards are all edible as are crawfish, frogs, toads, clams and snails. Many birds are edible, and some, like the wood grouse may be killed with rocks or clubs. All eggs are edible, so are many insects including grasshoppers, ants and termites, as well as some plants.

These are only general hints for survival. Before starting on that expedition into the wilderness you should learn to identify a number of edible roots, shoots, berries, seeds and nuts which grow in the area; learn what must be done with them before they can be eaten. Learn also what living creatures you may expect to find and how to capture them with snares, spears, clubs, and other native materials on hand.

WITH THE WILY ONES

Pursuit of the wily fish is so much a part of camping that the average camper considers his fishing tackle a part of his camping equipment, but the science of fishing is a subject in itself, one we cannot possibly cover here. However we can urge you to fish, and, as a camper, to learn how to clean, prepare and cook the fish you take.

Some edible fish have scales, others have none. Fish may be fried, baked, broiled or boiled; they may be cooked whole, or after entrails, head and fins have been removed, or as steaks; they may be scaled, skinned or filleted.

Small trout should be cooked whole. Just wipe off the slime, remove the entrails, wash, and broil or bake with lemon and butter. Small bass or perch may be scaled, skinned or filleted, then broiled in aluminum foil or fried in a pan. Large trout or pike should be steaked and baked. Walleye, that tasty pike-perch, should be filleted, and here's how.

Lay your fish on a smooth board, canoe paddle or other flat surface, and with a thin razor-sharp knife slice half of the fish's body away from its backbone from the gills to the tail but leave the skin attached to the tail. With the tail still attached lay this piece of fish on the board skin-side down, and with your knife held tightly against the board shave the meat free of the skin with one long stroke. Cut the few ribs away and you have a juicy fillet. Repeat for the other side.

CACHE IT, KEEP IT COOL

Safeguarding your food supply is not only a matter of protecting it from the ravages of weather and travel but of foiling robbers who would steal it. There are many four-footed food robbers in the woods who will raid your food with great glee if they have a chance. At night you will be wise to cache those food items which attract animals, or take them in your tent and prepare to repel raiders.

If you camp on an established site you can bet that some raccoons, skunks, weasels or dogs are watching your every move, waiting for an opportunity to grab your grub. When they get a whiff of your tasty cooking they drool too. In remote areas squirrels, porcupines, pack rats, bear and all their cousins are a menace to food supplies.

To frustrate these marauders cache your tasty smelly foods in a tree like the campers in the picture have done. With a rope hoist your pack high enough to be out of the reach of a bear and protect it from top assault with tin can baffles.

Food in odor-proof packages or cans is relatively safe stored in packs or wannigans next to your fireplace, for animals dislike fire and smoke.

Hungry bears will rip things apart to find food. They have been known to open cans with their teeth and suck out the contents.

In the heat of summer you may find it desirable to cool some of your food such as butter, puddings, or fresh-caught fish and game which you do not plan to cook. If you are near a stream or lake place the food in a covered pot and set this in the water where it will be out of direct sunlight. Hold it down with rocks.

Dig a hole in the ground if you are in the woods, place your pot in the hole and cover it with leafy boughs. The ground is generally much cooler than warm summer air. If you have a bit of cheese cloth or burlap you may fashion an evaporation cooler like the one shown on this page. In hot dry weather this will do an amazing job. To make one of these coolers suspend two pots one above the other. Place your food in the bottom pot, put some water in the top, and cover the entire rig with a wet cloth which has been anchored in the water with a rock. The cloth will act like a wick, and as the water evaporates the two pots and their contents will cool quite rapidly.

LET'S COOK

Because food can be a big morale booster—or a crusher —on any expedition, the wise camper should learn all he can about cooking through practice on his kitchen range before he tackles the job over an open fire. He realizes that camp cooks develop reputations quickly, for good food or for bad; he knows the good cook is one who turns out a reasonable variety of well-prepared food in ample quantity.

As a camp cook there are two primary problems: the organization of a kitchen and the control of heat. Through bitter experience you are apt to learn that the use of utensils must be scheduled; that food burns easily in the lightweight pots and skillets which are used for camping. Remember, you cannot turn down the fire with a twist of a knob; you may raise or lower your pots, but your primary heat regulators are the quantity and quality of the wood you use.

To be a successful camp cook you must learn the one real secret of open-fire cooking: use your fire as it burns. This means do your baking and boiling first while the fire burns high, and that the reflector oven must be ready from the start. Replenish the fire frequently with split firewood and a bit of softwood until your baking and boiling are done. Then flatten the fire to a bed of coals and start your simmering, broiling and frying.

When you work around a fire always wear gloves. An alert cook checks the condition of his fire and food frequently. He tests the temperature of his reflector oven by sprinkling a few drops of water on it. They should sizzle slightly, then dry quickly. With practice and experience he learns to whip up a tasty meal including pie or cake in ninety minutes or less, sometimes much less. The cooks on the opposite page are about to serve such a meal.

The good cook looks ahead too. He keeps a check on his food supplies and he works with his less experienced companions to show them a few tricks in the cooking trade. Before he retires for the night he places a pot of fruit on the dying campfire where it will simmer and soak. He mixes dry ingredients for breakfast cocoa, slices breakfast bacon and he protects a supply of firewood, kindling and tinder with a tarp.

SANITARY AND SAFE

City dwellers who are accustomed to the pure water which flows in endless quantity from faucets seldom recognize the fact that much of the water which sparkles in brooks, rivers and ponds is not safe to drink, but as campers we must think, and beware! When we camp in established areas safe water is always marked plainly. When we venture into the true wilderness water is always safe to drink; but in areas where other human beings live or camp water is often contaminated by human waste, and we must protect ourselves against disease and pollution in one of two ways: by the addition of Halazone Tablets or other chemical purifiers, or by boiling water for at least twenty minutes. Boiled water is flat, but its flavor may be restored by whipping a bit of air into it after it cools.

With such contamination in mind the true woodsman is doubly careful about the disposal of human waste from his own camping expedition. Where no toilet facilities are available he selects a spot off the trail, away from any water supply, and some distance away from his campsite to establish a latrine.

He digs a trench-like hole in the ground which may be refilled after usage or makes arrangement to cover all waste so it will not contaminate the countryside.

Other camp wastes such as garbage, wrappers and cans he disposes of by burning them and burying the remains. Cans which are burned before they are buried will decompose ten times as fast as unburned ones (page 80).

In general campers who start out healthy will return healthy if they make a fetish of cleanliness. Clean dishes are a must to prevent bacterial dysentery and the wise camper will not only wash his cooking and eating utensils after each meal, but boil them once a day and air dry them when possible.

The good camper takes pride in preservation of the wilderness, in removing all evidence of his camping, in leaving things exactly as he found them. The poor camper is easily identified for he leaves rubbish lying about, empty cans and bottles scattered, flowers and shrubs trampled, trees hacked and fire smouldering. Unfortunately he is much too conspicuous in our modern camping fraternity.

NEXT TO GODLINESS

Comes cleanliness—a most important part of camping which is neglected so often by an inexperienced camper, for he has been led to believe that campers, like their buckskin-shirted pioneer ancestors, never bother to wash themselves or change their clothes. Romantic stories of the past tell of the unwashed heroes who crossed the plains, but they omit descriptions of the hundreds who died on the way from filth and disease.

The modern camper who works hard and travels far becomes dirty and his clothes soil rapidly. He must wash his body and clothing frequently to be comfortable and to prevent those infectious diseases which always accompany filth such as boils and impetigo. When you are camping be sure you bathe and brush your teeth regularly. Take a bath daily whenever possible; change your underclothing daily and wash the dirty set right after you change. If you do these things you will eliminate the filth which can lead to infection and disaster. Like the Indians of old who took great pride in cleanliness, you will build your body into strong glowing health, and it will be a fit temple for your spirit.

BEFORE YOU HIT THE SACK

You have put in a long day of hard work on the trail. The evening meal is over, the dinner dishes done, and now as you sit leisurely by the fire sipping that last cup of tea, you may begin to enjoy the peace and solitude which a still night and a star-filled sky always bring. Soon you will be ready for sleep, that sound sleep which only the tired in body and spirit may enjoy. But before you crawl into your snug sleeping bag make sure that you are prepared for the night and the morning and the weather they may bring.

Check your tent to see that it will withstand strong winds and a deluge of rain. Check your clothing, equipment and food to see that they are properly protected. Close your car windows or bed your horses down for the night or stack your canoes in a spot where they will be safe. Douse your fire and make sure it is out so sparks cannot blow into the forest and set it afire during the night. Change into clean clothes and as you crawl into the tent take your paddle and ax so that porcupines cannot chew their salty handles. Now you are ready for that wonderful sleep.

SAFETY FIRST

Every real camper loves the challenge of adventure and the thrill of wilderness living, but he learns to temper his enthusiasm for boldness with the three time-tested camper-guardians: prevention, precaution and protection. He knows that he must stay whole and healthy to enjoy camping. Sickness or injury may endanger his life, deprive him of fun, and make him a burden to his companions. Because of this he makes every effort to prevent accidents, to protect himself and his equipment, and to be cautious in all his undertakings.

Experienced campers know that the greatest hazards to health and safety are camping tools, water, weather and disease. They know that cuts are the most prevalent type of injury, cuts which are caused by knives, axes and saws, by tin cans, sharp rocks and sticks, by fish hooks and other paraphernalia. A cut hand may be of little consequence in the city, but it is a distinct handicap in the woods. A wise camper keeps all of his cutting tools carefully sheathed when they are not in use, and he uses them only when they are truly needed. He is particularly wary of his ax because an ax bites hard, and a chopped leg is extremely serious when you are many miles from the nearest doctor or hospital. Use a knife and saw when you will—yes! but an ax—only when you must.

Another hazard which commands the full respect of every camper is water, for angry water can swallow up a camper in a flash and can drown him or dash him to pieces on the rocks. Never cross a large body of water in rough weather. Never paddle an overloaded canoe. Never swim alone. Never dive into unknown water; and you will remain a safe camper, one with a healthy respect for water.

There may be times when you cannot protect yourself from the torment of bad weather, when you must be wet and cold, but the camper who exposes himself needlessly to the elements is only a fool. Stay dry and warm when you can and protect yourself against the colds and bronchial infections which may spell disaster. Get plenty of sleep, eat well, stay dry and you will build your health while camping, not tear it down.

FIRST AID

When the best program of precaution and safety fails to prevent accident or illness you must fall back to your second line of defense: your first-aid kit, and you must know the basic principles of first aid to help a companion in distress. Prepare for this eventuality by studying a good course in first aid such as the excellent one sponsored by The American Red Cross, and by acquiring a kit of medical supplies adequate for the camping you will do.

Commercial first-aid kits are designed primarily to sell gauze and tape, and you unquestionably will be better equipped if you assemble your own. To start with, purchase a sturdy waterproof box. A 30- or 50-calibre ammunition box with a sound gasket, available in many surplus stores, will fit the bill nicely. It is tough and has a lid which locks tightly. Then procure the basic essentials: adhesive bandages, adhesive tape, gauze bandages, gauze pads, cotton, cotton balls, surgical soap, antibiotic ointment, pointed scissors, pointed tweezers, aspirin tablets and alcohol and you are ready for business.

These limited supplies will provide adequate first-aid protection for a trip through the national parks by auto or a day or two in the woods.

If your expedition is heading for a wilderness area where it may be out of contact with civilization and medical care for a period of days and perhaps weeks, then the list of necessary medical supplies will be quite extensive and you should consult your family physician to determine your needs. One thing you must have is a good book such as *The American Red Cross Text Book on First Aid,* and you should familiarize yourself with treatment recommended for the calamities which are most prevalent among campers. These would include cuts, scratches and infections; bites, blisters and burns; colds, sore throat and dysentery; foreign body in the eye, fish hook in the skin and fractures.

If you have been an iodine and merthiolate fan for many years, you may find it difficult to accept the modern use of a good surgical soap such as Physohex in their stead, but this is a wiser treatment for cuts and wounds and will promote more rapid healing. Once again, this emphasizes the fact that cleanliness is the greatest preventive weapon in the camper's arsenal.

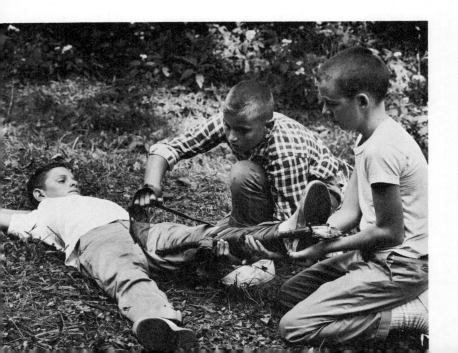

EMERGENCIES

The vast majority of all camping expeditions begin happily and end the same way, but there are some which will run into real trouble of an emergency nature. Before he departs the experienced camper anticipates this possibility with a careful study of all the safety valves in his camping area, the places where he may seek help. These include railroads, highways, police and ranger stations, mining, logging and prospecting camps, and resorts. He tries to consider the various emergencies he may face and the action called for by each.

Major physical hurts, such as a broken leg, are emergencies which call for first aid and something more: a well-conceived plan to move the patient to medical help or bring it to him. When one of your companions suffers a bad fracture immobilize it at once with a securely wrapped splint made from saplings, boards, strips of blanket, or the first thing at hand. Treat the patient for shock, then decide whether you should move him or bring help to him.

If one of your companions runs into trouble in the water and begins to drown, get him out as fast as possible, and if his breathing has stopped or is labored, begin mouth-to-mouth resuscitation immediately. Do not wait to get him ashore or carry him to a bench. Seconds count. When he starts to breathe treat him for shock and make him warm.

You may never know the awesome fear of facing wild fire in the woods, but if you do, you will never forget it, and you must act quickly. If the fire is a small one, you must fight it with every weapon at your command, with axes, saws and shovels, with pots of water if water is available. If the fire is already a towering giant and moving toward you, a hasty retreat is in order. Your life will depend upon your ability to move quickly and think clearly. You should head for water if there is any about, otherwise for the nearest large open space, a cave or a canyon. Grab some clothes for protection from the heat and ash, and a towel to filter the smoke.

When lost or trapped by a blizzard—stay put if there is any chance that others may find you. Conserve your strength and send up two columns of smoke from two small fires to call for help.

PESTS THERE ARE

When you venture into the wilds you will come in contact with many creatures which inhabit this earth of ours. Most of them are quite friendly, but some are pests of the first order and you must learn to combat these if you expect to camp in comfort. Insects are the worst, insects of all kinds, but mosquitoes form the shock troops; they are ably reinforced by chiggers, ticks, gnats, scorpions and flies in a zillion forms.

Grizzled old timers used to depend on rancid bear grease and a coat of dirt to ward off the swarms of mosquitoes and other insects, but in many instances the bear grease and dirt were worse than the pests themselves. Today the camper depends upon clothing and netting for his primary protection. This he fortifies with insect repellents and sprays, and a knowledge of the habits of his enemies.

If flies are prevalent in the tropics; they are overpowering in the North Country. The "bulldogs" of the North bite off big chunks before they fly away. Gloves and head nets are the best protection against flies.

Ticks enjoy a short but bothersome season, they are most prevalent in grass lands. Do not pluck a buried tick from your body for his head will remain in your hide and cause an infection. Just apply heat or some tobacco juice to him and he will back out on his own. Bee stings are exceptionally bad for some people. They may cause severe swelling, unconsciousness and even death. Beware of hornets, rock bees and wasps in the woods. Midges, gnats and noseeums can penetrate the finest netting. Repellents and sprays are the best defense against them.

Among the four-legged pests, raccoons, bears, mice, rats, skunks and porcupines are the most obnoxious. Be on the lookout for rabid animals, particularly skunks, which may attack you without provocation. A skunk is fearsome anyway. Don't push one or he will push back—with his tail. Firecrackers make excellent bear-discouragers as do noise and fire in general.

Snakes, lizards and scorpions are a prime menace to campers in some areas. Boots and vermin-proof tents are the best protection. There are only four poisonous snakes in North America; the rattler, copperhead, cotton-mouth moccasin and coral snake.

AND THE RAINS CAME

Nothing adds more fun and adventure to a camping trip than a few rain showers, but good humor and wit will fade slowly into the soggy reality of living in the wet when the rain gods brew a steady downpour. After six or seven days of rain the real campers in a group can be easily identified for they are the ones who still have one set of dry clothes, a dry sleeping bag and a bit of dry humor to bolster morale.

Most of us can tolerate days of misery in wet clothing if we have some dry clothes and a dry sleeping bag for the campsite, but no one can live in the wet all day, sleep in a soggy bag at night and maintain his health and morale. Secret —keep your sleeping bag dry at all costs.

In rainy weather pitch your tent in a somewhat sheltered spot when possible, one which will drain well. Set up a tarp for cooking and build a small fire under it as soon as possible. This fire is your "Man Friday" in bad weather. It must brew your tea, cook your one-pot meal, dry more firewood, dry your clothes and keep you warm. That's quite a job for a small fire, but with tender care it will do what you ask. Just take a look at the one here.

BIRCH BARK AND BUCKSKIN

Modern inventions have improved the lot of the camper, but there are two of the old time-tested materials which still do a superior job: birch bark and buckskin.

Contrary to popular belief, Indian-tanned buckskin is not the skin of deer alone. It is more apt to be the tanned skin of a moose, buffalo, calf or goat, but it is still tanned in the same old way.

For the modern woodland camper, buckskin makes the best shirts and footwear available. It is warmer than any cloth of equal weight. It is windproof, tearproof and washable. It resists thorns and will not pick up stickers or burs. For complete instructions on how to make it, see Mason's *Woodcraft*.

The white birch tree provided food, shelter and the comforts of home for the woodland Indians of old. It can do the same for a camper today. Birch wood makes excellent coals for cooking and sturdy staves for snowshoes. The inner bark can be ground into an edible flour. The sap makes a tasty syrup base, and the outer bark may be used for shelter, baskets, plates, cooking pots, tinder, boxes and many other things.

GRILLED IT'S GREAT

There are few people who do not relish the tasty flavor which charcoal imparts to a wide variety of meats and other foods. Charcoal cooking is one of the best, simplest and most efficient ways to prepare food on the trail, particularly when traveling by auto which makes it so easy to transport a few bags of charcoal and a pair of lightweight collapsible grills.

Like the campers pictured here, you should try the All-American hamburger in your initial attempt at charcoal camp cooking. Then tackle some "mad dogs": hot dogs stuffed with a bit of sharp cheddar cheese which have been wrapped with bacon strips secured by toothpicks and grilled to a golden brown. Next try pork chops plain or stuffed, steaks, chicken, sliced ham, thick-sliced Canadian bacon, corn-n-butter wrapped in aluminum foil, lamb chops and foil-wrapped fish with butter and lemon. For a pièce de résistance do a trimmed whole tenderloin rubbed in butter—and turn it only once.

Here's a camp secret: Light charcoal—boil food and water directly on it—put it in grill and do meat. Take it out and heat dishwater on dying coals. Simple, isn't it?

BARBECUE BEATS THEM ALL

In essence, barbecuing is the art of roasting a whole fowl, whole animal or large piece of meat over hardwood coals while basting it with a savory sauce. No other method of cooking imparts such marvelous flavor to chicken, beef, lamb or pork, and when properly aged or tenderized wild birds and game turn out wonderfully, but much of the secret is in the sauce. Try these.

Barbecue Sauce for fowl: Blend 1 cup white wine, ¼ cup sugar, ¼ pound melted butter, 1 teaspoon prepared mustard, 1 dash Tabasco, 1 teaspoon salt, 3 tablespoons catsup. Keep warm while in use.

Barbecue Sauce for red meat: Brown 1 cup flour in ½ cup bacon grease. Transfer to a pot. Add 3 cups vinegar, 3 cups water, 1 can tomato soup, 1 tablespoon salt, ½ teaspoon pepper, 1 tablespoon Worcestershire, ½ cup chili sauce, 4 large onions finely chopped, 4 green peppers finely chopped. Stir constantly. Cook until onions and peppers are soft, then add 1 cup sugar.

One of the simplest ways to barbecue a bird or a small chunk of meat is to suspend it in front of a reflector fire or large tepee fire of hardwood with a piece of wire or damp string; to baste it occasionally with sauce, give it a spin so that it will turn slowly as it alternately winds and unwinds, and catch the drippings with a pan. When it is half done turn it over, as the camper on the opposite page, and finish roasting to a tantalizing golden brown.

Big barbecuing is a dramatic cooking adventure which starts everyone drooling long before the food is ready. It calls for a pit big enough to accommodate the meat, a rick or more of good hardwood, and some steel or wood spits and skewers. To barbecue two thirty-pound top-round roasts of beef dig a pit about two by three feet and a foot deep. In it build a large criss cross fire of hardwood. Be generous with the wood, and when the fire burns down to coals support the spitted roasts over the pit with a green log on each side. Turn the roasts constantly and baste them often with that good sauce. As cooking proceeds you must replenish the coals in the pit periodically from a second fire which reduces hardwood to embers. About five hours of good heat, constant turning and occasional basting should produce the most delicious beef you have ever eaten.

THE CAMPER-NATURALIST

Chances are you will not camp long before you become aware that our woods are filled with campers of all types, some well informed and devoted to outdoor living, others ignorant and a menace to themselves, their companions and their natural surroundings. It may take a number of years for you to realize that the seasoned camper is not a camper alone, but a student of the woods and a naturalist at heart.

The seasoned camper attains the distinguished rank of camper-naturalist through long experience, hard work, patience and understanding. He makes a thorough study of all the techniques a person must master to live comfortably in the open, and he finds great happiness in learning about his natural environment—the plants, trees and creatures, that share it with him. As a woodsman he takes delight in passing this knowledge on to other campers who want to learn the ways of the woods.

The seasoned camper looks with anger and disdain upon those who camp in utter ignorance and in so doing destroy the wilderness which he loves. They are epitomized by the offensive ne'er-do-wells who pile all of their paraphernalia into a plane, fly off to a remote lake in the northwoods where they proceed to hack the trees, trample the shrubs, scatter their cans and bottles about, leave dead fish to rot on the shore, and fly home with never a thought for the wilderness area they have ruined or the next camper who may happen along.

If you would like to be a camper-naturalist your best bet is to go camping with one. You will be amazed at what you may learn in a short while, and you will begin to understand why the good camper loves the woods and all that goes with it. If you must go it alone, patience and hard work will bring success. In lake country try building a crude blind from which to watch the wary beaver at work or see the deer as they come down to the shore for water. In the muskeg lands of the north be on the alert for moose tracks and moose. You may be lucky enough to hear a big bull bugling for his mate. In state parks keep your eye on the raccoon. If you bait him with a morsel you may see him wash it before he eats. One day you will find yourself enjoying the thrill and self assurance that come from being a part of the woodland community. Then you will know what the camper-naturalist gains from his journeys into the wilds.

In The Words of a Camper

bite   notch made by an ax blade as it cuts into a log

bow-saw   buck saw with a bow-shaped steel frame

buckskin   Indian-tanned skin of moose, buffalo, deer, calf or goat

cache   store food safely beyond the reach of predators

cant hook   wooden handle with a metal hook and dog on the end used in handling logs

cedar saw   one-man cross-cut saw for cutting small logs

Chippewa Kitchen   three or four legged frame-work of saplings with shelves used to support pots and utensils over a campfire

crane   two forked sticks and a sapling which support pots over a campfire

cruiser's ax   three-quarter size double-bitted ax

ditty bag   small cloth or plastic bag with drawstrings

Duluth Pack   large back pack of woodsman carried with harness and tumpline

fillet   meat taken from one side of a fish without bones

haversack   rectangular back pack made popular by scouts

hew   shape a piece of wood with an ax

hitch   knot that fastens a rope to another object

kerf   space made by a saw as it cuts through a log

lashing   rope binding used to fasten two or more saplings together

moccasin-pacs   soft leather shoes with hand-stitched vamps

pannikin   nesting bowl of tin or plastic used for soup, cereal or beverage

pemmican   emergency food of dried beef or venison mixed with berries and fat

pole ax   single-bitted ax with a hammer surface opposite the cutting edge

rick   stack of firewood measuring four feet by four feet by four feet

rucksack   form-fitting back pack with special straps and side pockets

skewer   long pin of steel or wood used for securing meat to a spit

snare   device, as a noose, for catching birds or small animals

snoose   snuff, extra effort to do a job

squaw wood   dead branches broken from standing trees for kindling

tumpline   piece of leather strap with seven-foot leather thong attached to each end used to carry heavy loads in the woods

wannigan   logging-camp kitchen, camper's food box or box used to transport food and cooking utensils

waugan stick   sapling or stick used to support cooking pots over a fire

Wendigo   mystic being which pursues trappers, loggers and campers in the woods